Called, Appointed and Anointed

Prepare Your Life to Be a
Vessel for the Anointing and Glory of God

CALLED, APPOINTED AND ANOINTED

Prepare Your Life to Be a
Vessel for the Anointing and Glory of God

by
Janny Grein

Foreword by Kenneth Copeland

Harrison House
Tulsa, Oklahoma

12 11 10 09 08   35 34 33 32 31 30 29 28 27 26

Called, Appointed and Anointed
Prepare Your Life to Be a
Vessel for the Anointing and Glory of God
ISBN 13: 978-0-89274-354-4
ISBN 10: 0-89274-354-9
Revised Copyright © 1996
Copyright © 1981 by Janny Grein
Janny Grein Ministries
P.O. Box 150959
Fort Worth, TX 76108

Published by Harrison House, Inc.
P.O. Box 35035
Tulsa, Oklahoma 74153

Contents

Foreword

A number of years ago the Lord spoke to me and said, *You are not just a singer of songs. I have called you to the ministry of the Psalmist. I will hold you responsible for that ministry.* From that day my ministry of music changed, and is still developing. I spent several years developing my preaching ministry of the Word during which time the Lord only allowed me to sing occasionally. Many times I wondered what it all meant and I longed for someone to teach me in this area. If only someone had written a book about the Psalmist ministry that answered the puzzling questions that seemed unanswerable. Thank God someone has written that book — someone who knows what she is talking about!

Gloria and I have watched Bill and Janny Grein grow in their walk of faith and ministry since they began. We've seen them go through the tough times and the good. We've seen them when they were up, and we've seen them when the enemy was trying to put them down. Through it all, they have been true to their love for God's Word. We've sat amazed and thrilled while Janny played and sang to the sick under the anointing of God's power. Beautiful! Powerful! Glorious!

Every person in God's Kingdom should read this book — not only those who are called to the ministry of music. Everyone should have an understanding of this ministry that God has placed in the body. We need to know how to receive through it. We need to know how to better treat those in our midst who are called to the Psalmist ministry. No ministry can function to its fullest without people who have the proper respect for that office of ministry.

It goes without saying that everyone called to any office of ministry should read it. Everyone called to the Psalmist ministry should carry it with them, along with their Bible everywhere they go. It should be read again and again. It's one of those things of the Spirit of God that something new will come from every time it's read.

God bless you as you work in the kingdom to meet the needs of the people.

Jesus is Lord!

Kenneth Copeland

CHAPTER 1

...

Called

...

Called
•••

The call of God is on your life even before you are born:
You are called to be saved. That's your first call; everyone has
that call. The Bible says that the gifts and callings of God are
irrevocable. (Romans 11:29). They cannot change. Once
God has put that call upon you, He'll never take it away. You
might not fulfill it, but God will never take it back.

Your first call is actually a command of God. It's not a
suggestion and it's not a wish. First Timothy 2:4 says that
God **...wishes all men to be saved....** Moses told the
Israelites, **I have set before you life and death...therefore
choose life** (Deuteronomy 30:19). You have a free will, so
God puts it before you, because He wants *you* to *choose* it.
But the commandment is, choose life!

The reason I know it's a commandment is because I
know there's a punishment for it if you don't do it. If it were
a suggestion or an invitation, there wouldn't be any penalty
for not choosing it. But there is a penalty: to live in eternal
darkness and separation from God.

Your spirit is eternal. Before you were born again, your
spirit was going to live eternally in darkness because you
didn't choose God. We look at ourselves as flesh and blood,

but we're really not; our body is just the tent we walk around in while on earth. We are spirit beings. Your spirit is going to live eternally, either with God or in darkness. So, your first call is to be saved.

CALLED TO SERVE
...

God places different calls on different men and women's lives to serve Him in the kingdom of God. Some people are called into the area of ministering through music.

Those whom He calls into this ministry should be well-trained with their tools and gifts. Their skills are usually developed before they answer the call into the ministry; before they even get saved.

You'll find out that most people who are in music have had years of musical training before they ever start turning it toward God. They got out of balance with music and either made it their god or what they wanted to attain through music became their god. Music was a tool, but they hadn't used it for the purpose for which God created it. Since they didn't have any knowledge of it, how could they use it for God?

Then one day they get saved and fall in love with God. Now, what do they to do with the talents God has already developed in them?

Most people, when they get saved, aren't called directly into a public ministry. We're all called to be ministers of reconciliation, to minister salvation to the lost and to minister to one another as brothers and sisters, through the Word of God. We know that. But most people are not called into a public ministry. However, I have never seen a person who was highly trained in music who didn't have the call of God on his life to minister. Now, most of the people I've seen haven't answered that call or have only gone a step or two with it, however, the call of God is irrevocably on them. Many musicians are just unaware of that call.

One Sunday morning at Rhema Bible Church in South Africa, the Word of the Lord came to me and said, *Tell every musician to get up out of their seat and run down to the front.* I told them. I didn't qualify it. I didn't explain it. I just said it.

About 20 people popped up out of their seats and came running forward. The Spirit of God told me to prophesy to them, and I did. I spoke of the gifts that had been given to them by God. Then God spoke sharply to them and said, *This night I require my gift back. This night I require my gift to be turned toward me.*

God told me to give my guitar (the only one I had with me in South Africa) to one of the young men. I gave him the guitar, and he began to weep.

The Lord spoke to that man and said, *You are going to be an ambassador from this church to go out and do the good works of the Lord Jesus.*

That night, after my husband, Bill, preached, he gave an invitation for salvation. Every one of those musicians who was not saved, got saved and filled with the Holy Ghost. The call of God was already on their lives, but now they had been made aware of it.

Two months after I returned to the United States I received a letter from the young man I had given my guitar to, saying he had completely sold out to God. Today, he is the leader of a very famous rock-and-roll group in South Africa. He and his whole group have committed their lives to the Lord, and they are all out ministering from that church.

I have seen many people in the world doing the work of the Lord, and they aren't even saved! They're just doing it as a business. My husband used to design album covers for a lot of southern gospel singers. Some of them would be in the studio smoking and telling raunchy stories. At the time it didn't bother me, because I was also a sinner. I would look at them and think, *These guys aren't any different than I am. Why do I need what they have?*

Then I got saved and filled with the Holy Ghost. When they would come into the studio, I would walk up to them, throw my arms around them and say, "Guess what happened to me! I received Jesus in my heart!" I thought anybody who did anything in the name of Jesus was okay. They would push me away and say, "Oh, is that right?"

I was deeply hurt inside. It didn't even dawn on me that you could sing gospel music and not be saved! It was then I realized that God had called these people, and they had a desire to serve Him, but singing gospel music was the only part of their calling they had fulfilled.

There is a God gap inside all of us and only God can fill it. We try to fill it with all kinds of junk—music is one of them; school is another; business success is another. It doesn't matter what you try, there is only one thing that fits comfortably in there, and that is the Spirit of God.

One of the things the devil has done is taken all the tools designed to worship God and perverted them and distracted people with them. He has turned their attention on the things of this world, and made people fall in love with themselves and false gods.

In the fourth chapter of Mark, the distraction of the ages is one of the things named that comes to steal the Word of God once it has been planted in a heart. Music is one of the distractions of the ages when it is not used to glorify God. I'll be so frank as to say that anything in music that isn't directed toward encouraging you to think on things which are above, *anything that doesn't turn your spirit, soul and body toward God is of the devil.*

Music is used by the world to seduce, to destroy and to manipulate. I don't care if it is nice sweet music. They play nice sweet music in the grocery store. Do you know why they use music in the grocery store? Do you think it is to make you feel good? No! It is to relax you so that you'll spend more time in the store and buy more merchandise. That music isn't nice, and it isn't sweet. God is sweet. Music isn't sweet unless it puts your mind on God.

For the rest, brethren, whatever is true, whatever is worthy of reverence and is honorable and seemly, whatever is just, whatever is pure, whatever is lovely and loveable, whatever is kind and winsome and gracious, if there is any virtue and excellence, if there is anything worthy of praise, think on and weigh and take account of these things [fix your minds on them].

Philippians 4:8

5

Those are the things you should think on. Music that does not direct your thoughts to God is not worth listening to.

Perhaps you say, "I don't listen to rock-and-roll. But there isn't any good Christian music I can listen to."

Well, you are not supposed to be entertained when you listen to Christian music. It is supposed to be something that relieves your spirit, soul and body of the heaviness of the day and puts your mind toward God. It should remind you of how much you love God and how much God loves you. If the music you are listening to doesn't do that, then it is not worth listening to.

A TIME OF PREPARATION
...

At the beginning of any music ministry there needs to be a time of preparation. If a person is a skilled musician who has played for years outside of the kingdom of God, and then gets saved, he needs preparation before he is thrust back in front of people. Let me give you an example.

I know of two very famous performers. They both got saved, and they both love God. When one of them got saved, he was immediately thrust out in front of audiences. He does concerts all the time, sings many of his old secular songs and looks pretty much the same as he did before he got saved. Many of the Christians get up in the middle of his concerts and boo him and walk out. He is embittered against Christians and against the church. He needs prayer, help and support. His mind simply is not renewed to what God has done. He's a brother in the Lord, but he got thrust into the public eye when he was still a baby and before he was ready.

The other performer stayed hidden away for about eighteen months, doing nothing but reading the Bible and going to church. His brothers and sisters protected him from being thrust forward and manipulated by the press. He was already adept musically, but there was a time of preparation for him to fulfill the call that God had placed on his life and that time of preparation took place within his own church. When he resumed his concert schedule, he was determined to sing only those songs which glorify God. He would not sing any songs from his old lifestyle, and all he talked about is what God had done for him and how Jesus had changed his life. His former followers, thousands of them, came to hear his old songs. Some of them left because the Word offended them, but many saw a new rock star living for Jesus and that changed their lives, too.

Now, what's the difference? They both love God and God loves them both.

The difference is in being prepared and grounded for the call. There is an apprenticeship period we must experience as ministers of the Gospel; a time of preparation; a time of learning the tools of our ministry. The first and most important thing we learn, the very foundation we establish for our new life, is the Word of God. We must gain spiritual insight and understanding of God's will for our life through the study and application of His Word. Secondly, we must work with the Holy Spirit to develop and to perfect whatever skill God has given to us. Whether musical, oratorical, intercession, helps, giving or any other skill, God demands a quality of excellence from us, His ministers, as we imitate Him before the people.

During this time of apprenticeship and preparation we learn to communicate the Gospel. We learn how to grow in relationship with others and how to minister through our gift.

When you read about the musicians in the Old Testament, they often went *before* the soldiers. That's frontline warfare. A lot of injuries take place on the battlefield if you're not prepared and girded properly.

No matter what call God has on your life, no matter how excited you are about it, or how much you want to please God, if you don't get grounded in the Word of God, you're going to fail. Everything you do will slip and slide around. You may have a few minor successes but nothing compared to what God wants. The Word says,

> **This Book of the Law shall not depart out of your mouth, but you shall meditate on it day and night, that you may observe and do according to all that is written in it. For then you shall make your way prosperous, and then you shall deal wisely and have good success.**
>
> **Joshua 1:8**

There is an expression, *practice at home*, and that's a good idea. That's what I did. I sat before my church of a thousand people and forgot the words, cried, was unable to finish a sentence without muttering, and yet everyone loved me. They never criticized me, because they were my people; that was my home. They knew me when I was a sinner. They had seen what God had done in my life. They loved me and prayed for me and encouraged me so that I could go out in front of someone else and do what God wanted me to do.

This is a necessary time of preparation. This time is more accurately called discipleship. (It's not called shepherding. Jesus is the Lord, and the Lord is my only Shepherd. No earthly shepherd is my lord). It is biblical to submit one to another. You will never have any authority if you will not submit to authority. You have to be under authority to be in authority. I have no fear of submitting to authority; I will always do what God tells me to do. Many times God will send men and women along your path to help you to do what God tells you to do better and more quickly. If you will listen to them and submit to them—no matter how difficult it seems at the time—you can avoid a lot of problems.

You won't be prepared for your calling if you're not discipled in the Word of God. And you won't be discipled in the Word of God if you're not hooked in somewhere. That place really should be a good local church in your area that teaches the uncompromising Word of God. The local church will gain more power in the community if people will submit themselves to it and disciple themselves in the teaching of the Word. The whole community can be won through the local church.

Now some people say, "The whole body of Christ is my church."

That's deception. If you're not submitted to anything, then nothing is your church. You're not even submitted to God, because God says to get into a local church. (Hebrews 10:25). You see, there has to be a commitment, a quality decision you've made to submit to God's way of doing things. Determine to put old things aside and put on the new man and flow into maturity that so you can walk in the footsteps of Jesus.

Early in our ministry, we were living in an old tin trailer. We didn't have anything to eat or any furniture to sit on. We were learning to believe God, and God met our needs miraculously.

God put us in Kenneth and Gloria Copeland's heart and they discipled us in the Word. They sent us many of their tapes and kept in touch with us often to encourage us.

People came to our door at dinnertime with grocery sacks full of food for us. The church even paid our rent once. They knew we were seeking God and learning about the ways of God, and they determined to take care of us until we got to the point that we could take care of ourselves. They didn't require or expect anything back except the love of God and obedience to the will of God. That's what they expected and that's what they spoke over us, all the time.

We spent our time—weeks, months—reading the Bible, listening to tapes, fasting and seeking the ways of God. In the beginning, we studied and prepared for our call. We learned to walk in faith, and how to believe God in our own lives, as we were prepared to minister to others.

In the ministry of music, as in other areas of ministry, a lot of people don't want to pay the price of waiting on God.

Unless you're willing to pay it, however, you're never going to be used the way you want to be used, much less the way God wants to use you.

Most musicians have a talent and a gift and are very excited about Jesus when they get saved and filled with the Holy Spirit. But they don't want to wait on God to be renewed in their minds with the Word of God so they can be good warriors. Most of them just don't realize that there are heavy battles ahead, and they aren't going to be able to handle them with flesh and blood. You can't forget, however, that our battles are in the spirit realm, and that's why you've got to get everything straight before you can really use the gifts and skills God has given you in the natural world.

To give you an example, I was recently ministering in a church where there was a heavy oppression that just wouldn't lift. In the end it did leave, but only because we were patient enough to wait it out and stay persistent in the spirit until we won.

Years ago, I made a quality decision in this ministry that I didn't care how long it took to bring deliverance to somebody or how long God wanted me to stand and do something, or how people criticized me, or what they said, even if it was a lot of people. I don't care anymore. You've got to get to the same point if you're going to please God. I've gotten past the point of caring what men think, and I only care what God says to do. I'll do what God tells me to do even if only one person gets blessed. You don't need to be concerned about everybody, because not everybody wants to, or is ready to receive from God.

What I want you to see is that you've got to go for the one person God wants. Even if only one person gets free by you doing what God says to do, be faithful to what He says, no matter what it looks like and no matter how uncomfortable it feels. But you won't be prepared for your call if you haven't been hooked up somewhere and made yourself a disciple in the Word of God.

I really have to emphasize the need for you to be committed to a local church that preaches and teaches the uncompromising Word of God. People who want to be spiritual lone rangers are the ones who get picked off by the enemy, and it's the same in music as in anything else.

What eventually happens to most really good musicians who won't pay the price to prepare spiritually is that they wind up going back to secular music. Why? Because there is no commitment; no quality decision in anything they've done in the spirit. They're like a lot of Christians who fit Paul's description of the spiritual babies in First Corinthians 3; spiritual babies who just drift around and float from one thing to another, going here tonight and there next week.

You have heard people say, "I don't like the way he talks;" "I like him because he brings his whole family;" or, "I like him because the benches tremble when he preaches." That was what the people were doing in Corinth. It's time to stop being babies; it's time to just put those things aside. What you've got to do before you even think of ministry is to make that quality choice to put on the new man. If you want to flow into something, then just flow into maturity so you can fill the footsteps of Jesus.

I really want you to understand this, especially if you're called into the music ministry, because God is tired of us messing around when He's given us so much. He's going to require a return from us because He doesn't like to lose out on His investments. If He finds a shirker, He'll try to get the slack out of him. If He can't do that, then He'll just move on to someone else who wants to do what He says. If you don't want to do things His way, then you can get prepared to stay at home. It's harder, but you can do it that way. You have to get an understanding of commitment. Get ahold of the whole spiritual picture—not just your music—or you're not going to succeed.

It really is simple. All you have to do is submit yourself to the Word of God, submit yourself to one another, and get prepared for your calling. Another thing you need to do is to be around someone who is in the ministry you're called to. If you're called to be a singer or a praiser of God with music, then you need to be around somebody who does the same thing you're called to do; and you need to learn to imitate one who is doing it well.

Pattern yourselves after me, [follow my example],
as I imitate and follow Christ (the Messiah).
1 Corinthians 11:1

When we imitate others in the ministry, we're really just imitating God.

Now, don't get the wrong idea about what I'm saying. It's natural for children to imitate their mother or father while they're growing up, isn't it? Well, as you grow up spiritually, the same thing happens to you and as you continue to grow, your own personality begins to take over. Then when you've got everything all together for yourself, the things that really aren't you just drop away.

PURITY OF MOTIVES
...

One of the key things that will determine whether you succeed or fail with God is the purity of your motives.

I remember the time we had eight people on our staff. They all loved God. You know how it is. Every one of them loved God and wanted to serve Him. But one by one, you could see where their commitment was: it was really in exalting themselves. Five out of the eight were out to exalt themselves and get their own ministries going. You've got to watch that motive carefully. Some of the people who were working for us got the idea that God had called them to do what we were doing, only better than we were doing it. There is always someone who thinks they can do what you're doing better than you can.

What we've had to do is to set up guidelines, and it's important for you to understand this. When you get going in your ministry, you'll have people come up to you and say what people have said to us, "God wants me to come and do this for you." You have to know what God has told you, and that vision has to be burning in your hearts as well as theirs if there is going to be harmony between you.

If God has called you, and you've been diligent to prepare for that calling, He's also the One who is going to call you to account for that gift and calling. So you'd better be a wise and zealous steward over your ministry. You should read the parable of the talents in Matthew 25 and get serious about what God has put in your heart as an investment for His kingdom. He'll ask you about it, so you'd better be ready to account for what you've done with it.

The key to how much your talent will increase lies in your commitment.

One big learning experience in our ministry came when a man came to work for us in the ministry of helps. It did not work out well. The reason it didn't work is that when we commit responsibility to someone, we commit it, and if that person doesn't do his job, it doesn't get done.

If someone is supposed to carry my guitar and put it on my music stand, when I get ready to minister in song, I'll just go up there and look at the guitar stand. Now, if the guitar is supposed to be there and it isn't, I won't go to the back of the church and pick it up; I'll just stand there and wait. Why? Because I've given that responsibility to someone else. Sure, you can do another man's job, but he won't learn about responsibility if you do.

Well, this person just didn't get things done, and yet he really thought that he was doing things better than everybody else. About a month before he was going to leave, God said to me, "He's going to be leaving, so prepare yourself for this hole." So we started preparing someone else to do what he was doing.

One day we came into the office, and I said, "When are you leaving?"

He was surprised I knew and said, "Well...well...I guess next week will be my last week."

I said, "I see. Did you plan on giving any notice?" You see, he had been in the ministry of helps, but he hadn't learned much about that yet.

He said, "Well, God has given me a bigger vision." He then went on to explain his vision. It was the same vision we had, but there was a preparation needed to fulfill it.

God will show you a vision, and it's like a big football game. You might as well go eat your victory dinner now, because you're going to win; but you're still going to have to play the game. Somebody is going to have to carry the ball from one end of the field to the other. That's the rule of the game.

It doesn't really matter if you're the best team, you still have to follow the rules, and that's the way it goes. If you don't run with the vision God gave you—from the beginning to the end—you won't fulfill it, someone else will. You'll see it and want to be a part of it—and you might even know exactly what is going to happen—but you'll never fulfill the vision if you're not willing to run the whole game according to the rules.

Most young ministers called to music aren't willing to be patient, diligent and disciplined until God tells them to step out.

You really have to get clear about God. He's a success in everything He does. Everything He does will succeed because He's disciplined and moves step by step.

We need to see that there has to be a time of apprenticeship in the ministry just like there is in a trade in the world. When you have learned the tools of the Word and the Spirit, as well as the skills of your music, then you'll be ready. There has to be the parallel development of the spiritual and musical ability of the person called to minister.

If your musical skill overbalances your skill in yielding to the Word and the Holy Spirit, you'll have minor victories, and yes, Jesus will be praised, but you won't do what God wants you to do. If the Word isn't the sword in your mouth, then you won't destroy the works of the devil like God wants you to. And you had better well be ready, because you're going to have trouble.

After you realize that you're called, you'll need to spend time learning how to communicate the Gospel effectively; to learn how to have patience and a pure heart while you're learning. There is a time when you're going to have to grow and there's a time when things just have to come together for you.

I'm really adamant about music and what it's used for, because I've spent time being quiet before God, and studying and meditating on the Word to find out what the function of music is. There is no purpose for music outside of the kingdom of God.

I have found that knowledge plus application brings wisdom and understanding. Having put the principles of the Word in action musically, I have seen the same signs and wonders that occur when the Word is preached.

People who are called to minister to the Lord in music have to have the same dedication as the priests in the Old Testament. Musicians then were considered just as holy as the priests. They had to be sanctified just like the priests, and they had to be just as courageous as the warriors. They went before the battle rejoicing.

We have got to take this calling with just as much seriousness and be just as committed to it.

CHAPTER 2

•••

Appointed

•••

Appointed
• • •

EXCELLENCE FIRST
• • •

God demands excellence in whatever you do for Him. If you are called to be a preacher, but haven't really been grounded in the Word or haven't learned how to communicate the love of God you know is inside of you, what good can you do? Well, the same is true in music.

I have a lot of people come up to me and tell me they can play this or that and ask me what they should do with it. Well, if you aren't called of God into public ministry just praise God on your own time, with brothers and sisters fellowshipping in His presence. You know there is an expression, *Just because you stand in the garage doesn't make you a car.* Well, the same goes for music. Just because you sing or play an instrument doesn't mean that you should stand up in church and do it.

I don't know if you've ever heard the phrase that's around the music business, but it says, *It's good enough for gospel.* You hear those people say, "We don't have to clean it up too much; it's good enough for gospel."

The first thing you ought to know is that it isn't good to try to be what you aren't. You have to be good at what God calls you to do, and you shouldn't do what you aren't good at if God hasn't called you to do it. Look at the Old Testament. Chenaniah was one of the singers appointed by David to minister unto the Lord, and he was the best they had.

> **Chenaniah, leader of the Levites in singing, was put in charge of carrying the ark and lifting up song. He instructed about these matters because he was skilled and able.**
>
> **1 Chronicles 15:22**

You are required to take everything that God has given you and spend the time necessary to be good at what you do. God demands that. He demands excellence. Don't ever let anybody talk you out of that. Excellence of ministry is the least you can give God, because everything you do is reflecting His glory. If you aren't doing it to the best of your ability, then you're failing in what God has called you to do. Take hold of the fact that *God doesn't make failures*, and He not only programmed you for success, but He has given you the avenues to do what He expects of you. He won't ask you to do what you can't do without His help, so give Him your best effort.

You should never get the idea that because there is an apprenticeship period in your ministry that you shouldn't do your very best during that time. Remember that God is shaping you for your calling. He will shape you and prepare you to be shot out like an arrow.

Then, when you are ready, God will appoint you to a task. He won't appoint you before you're ready. He might

give you a picture of it—a vision of what you are going to
do—but He is never going to give you the word, *Go*, until
you are ready to do it.

Do you know why?

Because He doesn't want you to fail. He wants you to be
a success in everything you do. He knows that with the right
groundwork and the right preparation, you can make it.
That is why He said in 2 Timothy 2:15:

> **Study and be eager and do your utmost to
> present yourself to God approved (tested by
> trials), a workman who has no cause to be
> ashamed, correctly analyzing and accurately
> dividing [rightly handling and skillfully teaching]
> the Word of Truth.**

That means, do the best that you can do to present
yourself to God, approved. In other words, God isn't going
to wave a little wand down on you to make you perfect. The
Bible says you have to work out your own salvation in fear
and trembling. (Philippians 2:12). Part of that is to ground
yourself in God's Word. Show that you are willing to submit
yourself to God and to authority by putting off the way you
think and putting on the way He thinks.

Maybe the hardest part of putting on God's way of
thinking is to wait for Him to let you know when you're
ready to do what He's told you to do. First Peter 5:6 says:

> **Therefore humble yourselves** [actually put off
> your way of thinking and think like God] **under the
> mighty hand of God, that in due time He may
> exalt you.**

If you clothe yourself with God's Word and exalt His Word...His Word will exalt you!

Many people wonder, *Why isn't my music ministry going anywhere? Why isn't my teaching ministry going anywhere? Why isn't my preaching ministry advancing? Why doesn't my church get behind me? I know God has called me to do this.* Have you humbled yourself? Have you put off your thinking and put on God's thinking? God says that in the perfect, exact, right timing, He will lift you up, if you are thinking and acting His way.

But, if you're thinking and acting your way, it's going to take a long time. You will be fretting and worrying and starving the whole time you wait. The next verse says:

> **Casting the whole of your care [all your anxieties, all your worries, all your concerns, once and for all] on Him, for He cares for you affectionately and cares about you watchfully.**
>
> **1 Peter 5:7**

You can't do that if you don't humble yourself under the mighty hand of God. You can't be carefree; you can't let all your troubles go if you're thinking like you want to think.

When you come to the time when you know that God has not only called you but that He's appointing you, you have to balance out His abilities and your inabilities and rest on His strength. The man who is falsely humble will back away from God's appointment by saying he isn't worthy of it.

He might quote the first half of 1 Corinthians 2:16 saying we can't know God's mind, forgetting that the last half of that verse is there to enable us, reminding us that we do have the mind of Christ. If you walk by God's Word, then you will be humbling yourself under His hand, and you will have the mind of Christ.

Some people seem to think God is saying, *Humble yourself under My hand, and then you can raise yourself up.* There seems to be a contradiction in humbling yourself and being strong in the Lord, but there isn't. A meek man isn't a man who is weak. He's one who knows his mind and has God's plan and sets his face like a flint to get there.

The man who has God's mind doesn't have to fight and struggle and push and be brash and make his own demands all the time. He knows when to lay back and take in God's rest, and when to be aggressive and take the kingdom by force. So wisdom about when to receive from God by waiting on Him to move and when to move forcefully against the devil is part of being an excellent minister, no matter what your calling is.

ACCORDING TO THE WORD
...

And said to them, You are the heads of the fathers' houses of the Levites; sanctify yourselves, both you and your brethren, that you may bring up the ark of the Lord, the God of Israel, to the place that I have prepared for it.

For because you bore it not [as God directed] at the first, the Lord our God broke forth upon us—because we did not seek Him in the way He ordained.

> So the priests and the Levites sanctified themselves to bring up the ark of the Lord, the God of Israel.
>
> The Levites carried the ark of God on their shoulders with the poles, as Moses commanded by the word of the Lord.
>
> David told the chief Levites to appoint their brethren the singers with instruments of music—harps, lyres and cymbals—to play loudly and lift up their voices with joy.
>
> 1 Chronicles 15:12-16

David was giving the instructions the Lord had given to him about who was to carry the ark of the covenant, and who was to minister to Him. Notice how everything they did concerning the ark of the covenant was according to the Word of the Lord.

Verses 17 and 18 of that chapter specify two degrees, or classes, of appointments. There is a divine order that God has set up. That doesn't mean one is less worthy or less important than the other. This is just their position in the kingdom of God.

It is like the family. There is the husband who is the pastor of the home and the teacher of the children. There is the wife who is also a teacher of the children and the help-meet of the husband. Then there are the children who are to obey their parents so that their days may be long on the earth. This is the order of the home.

If you don't follow that divine order, you will be messed up, your ministry will get messed up and everyone you touch will get messed up. They will see you and copy you. As ministers of the gospel we are commanded to have our lives in order and to walk holy, upright and blameless before the people—without reproach.

I pray that everyone in the church would meditate on the biblical examples of praise and worship. Maybe they'd see how far we've come from the glory of God in praise and worship in some of our assemblies.

During David's time, every day, all day long, people were appointed to sing and praise God. That was their job. That was their appointment. God had groomed them. They were skillful in their tasks. God had called them, and they waited on God. Then God anointed David, and David pointed them out as he recognized the call of God upon their lives. He said, "You will be the chief singer. You will play the cymbals. You will do this, and you will do that. You will preside over this section; you over that one. You will be purified like the priests; you will be cleansed. You will have to go through the same ritual. You have the same responsibility."

There is something about the glory of God in the Old Covenant that excites me when I read of it. I read the stories of the glory cloud descending and the enemy slaying themselves. The priests were in the temple worshipping God in one accord when the glory of God came in like a cloud, and they were not able to stand. Wow!

But think of it now. We are living in a new day, a new covenant. The glory of God does not just rest on us, it is on us and in us as Christ and the anointing dwells in us. Such power—the same power that raised Jesus from the dead—

dwells in you and me and will break any yoke of bondage if administered properly.

As we come into one accord and lift our hearts to God in love and adoration, He dwells in the midst of our praise. He isn't there just to make us feel good either—He's there to lift up our heads, our minds, our souls and even our bodies to a new and higher way of living, praise God. Now, that's exciting!

The power of God is in us right now, and it comes to full fruition in response to our obedience and to our diligence in rightly dividing the Word of God. Walking in God's glory carries a heavy responsibility, but as ministers who want to reflect that glory that He might be magnified, we have no choice but to sanctify ourselves in our ministry to Him.

> **But in a great house there are not only vessels of gold and silver but also [utensils] of wood and earthenware, and some for honorable and noble [use] and some for menial and ignoble [use].**
>
> **So whoever cleanses himself [from what is ignoble and unclean, who separates himself from contact with contaminating and corrupting influences] will [then himself] be a vessel set apart and useful for honorable and noble purposes, consecrated and profitable to the Master, fit and ready for any good work.**
>
> **2 Timothy 2:20-21**

The decision is yours. I believe, in your heart, you desire to be profitable for *every good work* and that will come to pass as you obey the Word of God.

APPOINTED TO A TASK
· · ·

As we look back at Chenaniah, we recall that he was appointed because he was skilled and able. He had studied, and he was approved. He had been called, and he had served his apprenticeship. As soon as he was ready, God appointed him and gave him a task. David singled him out. He said, "God told me to appoint you to carry the ark and to be the leader of the singers." He taught the others how to carry the ark, where to put it, which direction it had to face, everything.

Because he respected God's Word and had submitted to an authority, he was raised to a position of authority himself. He had a tremendous job!

You should never overlook the technical side of music. We have to be skilled and able, like Chenaniah, if we want to have God's approval and appointment. Chenaniah was technically the best. The Bible doesn't say anything about his spiritual attitude or sensitivity, but you know it had to be good or he wouldn't have been put there.

Do you see the balance in Chenaniah that has to be in the music ministry, or any other ministry for that matter? He fulfilled an important place in the whole nation of Israel and before God because he had done what would gain God's approval. He wasn't the king or prophet, and he didn't try to interfere with what they did. But what he did was as important to God's glory coming into the temple as anyone else's job or attitude of heart was.

It's like that today. You see someone who is singing gospel music, has sold 1,000,000 copies a week of their records and has been on national television. Then you don't hear about them anymore and somebody asks, "Who was that who sang such and such?" And you say, "Who?" They just disappear because they don't do it God's way. *What could have happened to him? He was really great.* God isn't interested in shooting stars. He's interested in guiding lights for people lost at sea. He needs people He can count on so others can find their way home.

If you have it in your heart to be a guiding light, then God will put you in position to be a star that can shine His glory out into all the earth for many who are lost. That was as much a part of Chenaniah's excellence as anything, and it should be yours too.

MINISTERING TO THE LORD
...

In the Old Testament, the musicians spent all day worshipping God—it was their job, and they received a share of the offerings given.

Today there should be a real effort by the church to encourage musicians by giving not only honor but also support to those chosen and appointed by God. As they are lifted up in the Spirit and before the body of Christ by God, others will dedicate themselves in the same way.

This is not to suggest all who play instruments are called of God. If the church doesn't hire the musicians anointed of God or encourage them to follow after God with their talents, then Satan will be there with opportunities and invitations that look really good and even very spiritual. His alternatives don't look like they would hurt at all. But then the musician finds himself out on a limb, and if he gets into playing worldly music again, he may even doubt his salvation.

One reason there aren't many good orchestras in churches today, or good temple musicians or psalmists, is that churches are too tight with their money. In the Old Testament, the priests were given the best, and the musicians were right in there with them. Today many have to go out to a secular job and come in at night totally unspiritual. They have had to work all day hassling the world. They've tried to keep their minds on God, but they just aren't ready to minister in the Spirit.

Musicians should be in the Spirit for three or more hours, worshipping, getting instructions and playing to the Lord, before they minister. Then you'd see what an anointed music ministry could be. Temple musicians in the local church who have devoted themselves to the call God has on their lives should be paid by that church once they have been recognized and appointed by their pastors.

When someone comes to a pastor and says, "I want to serve God. I want to play for God," that pastor should pray earnestly about it. Let them come. Tell them, "If you want to play for God, come in around 3 o'clock this afternoon. Nobody will be here then. Just express yourself toward God." If they come in and worship God, let them do it. Don't bother them anymore about doing anything else until they are ready or until God tells you to appoint them, if He does.

A lot of musicians don't want to do that because they just want to sing to people. That's how you know what's really in the person's heart. They think, *What good is it to sing if you can't sing in front of somebody?* Well, who is God? He is somebody. He is the one you are supposed to be singing to, anyway.

Many times before we go to minister some place, I'll go ahead and sit at the piano for two or three hours and just minister to the Lord and get the atmosphere ready. I like to charge the air with praise. I'll just keep singing, as the people come in. When they hear me playing and singing, they feel the presence of God and come in to worship and praise God.

Right there they are already with the Spirit of God. It doesn't take two or three hours to get them ready to receive the Word. They can worship and enjoy the presence of God, enjoy being in fellowship with one another. The problems of the day will just go away. If you're not prepared to do that, how can you lead somebody else into doing it?

I was not usually prepared. I would just hang around and talk to everybody before the services and visit. I loved to be with people and hear things that God was doing. Then I would get up and start singing, and it would take me half the service to flow into any kind of anointing at all.

God told me that I had to spend time before the service with Him—at least two or three hours—either in prayer or in ministering to Him in song. He told me to get away from everybody before the service, because I wouldn't do Him any good if I didn't.

You know, during those periods of time prior to a service I have received some outstanding songs from God. *By His Word,* and *Build Your House on the Rock* are among them. He shows me people who have needs that will be there and how to minister to them. It is a wonderful and intimate time with great rewards. Sometimes the time prior to the meeting is as exciting as the meeting!

If we want a continual flow of the Holy Spirit, we are going to have to set it up like God commanded us to set it up. The day is coming when the temple musicians are going to come into the temple (yes, you are the temple, but there is a place of worship called the temple) and worship God all day long. That will be their job. They'll worship God all day long. Then when people come in there will be such a difference.

If you are in music, you'd better get into the worship of God and begin instructing one another in psalms, hymns and spiritual songs. You will see the glory of God manifested if you will worship God right with the tools He has given you.

If you are a pastor of a church, when you delegate authority to someone, especially in the area of music, release it and let it go. Don't delegate it until you can let it go. Don't delegate it until that person has gone through an apprenticeship, until he is ready for the job. Then you appoint him to a task saying: "You are going to be my chief musician. We will call you the minister of music. You are going to organize what the Holy Ghost says to do. You are going to be responsible to direct the people to do it."

The chief musician takes his authority over the orchestra and says, "I have been appointed to direct you, under the leadership of the Holy Ghost. Now as the Holy Ghost tells me what to do, I am going to tell you, and you are going to do it."

Each person in the orchestra says, "I will do it. I believe you are a man of God, and when you say the Holy Ghost moves, whether I feel it or not, I will submit to your authority and I will do what you say."

Musicians: Be trained and ready when you are appointed. Pastors, the way to have confidence in them is to do what David did: Train your song leader in the Word. Let your leader train the orchestra. Get them all together so you are all doing the same thing out of one spirit and mind.

If you will read 1 Chronicles 16:8-36, you'll see that David gave instructions about what to sing and how to do it. He built them up in the Word of God. He reminded them of everything that God had done. It got them excited about God and what they had to do for God. Then David left them.

So David left Asaph and his brethren before the ark of the covenant of the Lord to minister before the ark continually, as each day's work required.

1 Chronicles 16:37

Worship was the job of the musicians, and they did it every day. David left them there because he trusted them not to dilute the Word; because they had been called of God: they had been trained. He appointed them, and they were able to do their task.

If you want the successful results David achieved, you've got to do it God's way, knowing and apprenticing people before you appoint them. A lot of pastors respond to the pressure of their need for musicians and take the first person who comes along. And so God can't use the church, not even the Word, the way He wants to because the people with the wrong attitude are up there playing before the Word is ministered.

It's also a lot harder for the anointing to flow through an untrained musician or someone who sings off key and keeps everybody wishing that they would just sit down. As a pastor, you have a big responsibility to recognize and train God's person to fulfill the needs in your church. Professionals who rely on their natural skills can be as bad as untrained musicians because either way, the Holy Spirit can be shut out. Musicians must go through all the steps we've outlined in order to fulfill any excellence of quality work for God.

FOR HIS KINGDOM AND GLORY
• • •

I want to share some things with you about anointed ministry, not because it happened while I was singing, but because the Holy Ghost will work in your ministry just as much as anybody else's if you'll do what He tells you to do.

First, I got saved because of worship. The people had been worshipping God and singing for an hour before I walked into the church. When I came in, a heaviness of love came over me, like a big, thick, soft blanket. I could hardly walk to my seat. I just began to weep and weep. I didn't know God from a boot. I just wept and wept. I looked around, and every time I started to think of something, I just wept. I got saved before they even preached. Can you see how strong the work of the Holy Ghost is under anointed music?

I was saved and filled with the Holy Ghost because the love of God was flowing and the anointing of God was so strong it broke the yoke of bondage that had imprisoned me.

Ministry to the body of Christ is a very important part of music. In Austin, Texas, a woman who was blind and in a school for the blind was sitting in the front row as I sang. We were just worshipping God and getting ready to receive the Word, just like the Bible says to do, and the lady began to see things—blurry. She wrote down on a piece of paper all she saw and what happened to her. She was healed.

You see, singing drives the devil crazy. One time, when I sang in Temple Terrace, Florida, there was a boy there possessed by an evil spirit. God told me to call him up and have him stand in front of me as I sang. He was so deteriorated by this spirit that he looked about fifty even though he was only about twenty years old. The two women who had brought him had to carry him up. He was so wasted away you could hardly see him sideways.

I began to sing, *The peace of God that passes all understanding will keep your heart and mind in Christ Jesus.* It drove the evil spirit crazy. I mean he looked like he would have loved to kill me. I just laughed and kept singing.

It took me about twenty minutes, but I just kept singing. Finally, he began to weep and went limp when the evil spirit left. He was saved and filled with the Holy Ghost. Then he sat down.

Norvel Hayes was with us that night and taught on worship. The boy took hold of what Norvel was saying, and his whole countenance changed completely that night.

In one meeting in Michigan, a woman had cataracts on her eyes that just fell off while I was singing. In Houston, Texas, a woman had a large tumor in her breast. We were praising God and edifying one another, and she felt the tumor move. She looked at her dress and couldn't see it, so she went to the restroom and examined herself. It was completely gone.

Forty people got healed at Lakewood church during the music ministry one night. I didn't have time to minister one-on-one to people, so I just told people in a certain section to stand up and receive their healing while I ministered to them.

The same thing happened at the Word of Faith Center in Farmer's Branch, Texas. People were healed of things such as blindness and deafness. One man who had been maimed in a wreck and had tremendous pain all down his body stood up and received total manifestation of his healing.

Another young girl who had been severly injured came to our meeting in Colorado. She had been jogging down the street and was struck by an automobile doing 60 miles per hour. The doctors told her it would take many operations for her to be able to walk and that she would never run again. At our meeting she was instantly and completely healed as I sang, *Don't give the devil an opportunity.* She threw down her crutches and began running around the church.

Another man, up in Michigan, had a steel pin in his leg completely disappear. He could bend his leg for the first time in years and had no pain. That gets exciting!

Since music is used for everything in the world, generally to get you to do something or buy something, we have to purify our music before God. God originally created musical ability, and it was meant only for His kingdom and glory. Except in God, there really isn't a place for music. As Christians, we ought to be pacesetters, just like God, not followers of the world.

Musicians aren't exempt from the high standards that God requires for every calling He has. God set that standard for us in Christ. A lot of musicians think they can get out of that, and they imitate the world. But there is no holiness in imitating what the world does.

I believe we're going to see a real boldness coming forth in music—a boldness to glorify God. But it will take sanctified and consecrated musicians full of the Holy Ghost, skilled and able ministers of the Word of God to do it.

CHAPTER 3

...

Anointed

...

Anointed

•••

We've talked about getting a good foundation in the Word of God so you can effectively communicate the Gospel. We've talked about going through an apprenticeship period to be prepared. You submit yourself to the authority of the one who is experienced and who has been walking in God's wisdom longer than you have so you can accelerate at a faster pace. He can teach you things, you can learn quickly, and then God can raise you up. If you don't know how to submit to authority, you will never know how to walk in authority and others will find it difficult to submit to you.

You have to experience everything that you do in life step by step. You can't skip from part A to part C, because if you try to jump over part B, you won't have a foundation for part C.

Your apprenticeship and discipleship period is the time when God is shaping you for a task. He wants you to be an able workman. We saw how David prepared himself and became an able workman. When he was appointed to his task, he was able to recognize the skills of musicians and place them in authority and appoint them for their tasks.

David knew his trade well, and he was a polished musician. But he also balanced his technical skills with spiritual knowledge. The two melted together, and God could use him both as a minister and as a leader.

Let's look at what the results of God's program were.

THE CLOUD OF GLORY
. . .

In Second Chronicles 5:11-14, we get a picture of what power an anointed ministry of music and praise ought to have.

> And when the priests had come out of the Holy Place—for all the priests present had sanctified themselves, separating themselves from everything that defiles, without regard to their divisions;
>
> And all the Levites who were singers—all of those of Asaph, Heman, and Jeduthum, with their sons and kinsmen, arrayed in fine linen, having cymbals, harps, and lyres—stood at the east end of the altar, and with them 120 priests blowing trumpets;
>
> And when the trumpeters and singers were joined in unison, making one sound to be heard in praising and thanking the Lord, and when they lifted up their voice with the trumpets and cymbals and other instruments for song and praised the Lord, saying, For He is good, for His mercy and loving-kindness endure forever, then the house of the Lord was filled with a cloud,
>
> So that the priests could not stand to minister because of the cloud, for the glory of the Lord filled the house of God.

I believe that this is the kind of anointing and ministry God wants the church to have today, but there are certain things you must do to achieve this. You have to have the desire to abide in the Word of God and have His Words abide in you. That kind of glory should not only be in the congregation, but it should be out in the streets as well.

God wants that holy boldness to come over you so that you stand in the place of Jesus on this earth. Then you will see the anointing of God break the yoke on those held in bondage. You will need that anointing to do it, to accompany whatever you are skilled at. You are going to have to have that anointing to bring it about.

But do you also know that it's not going to be dealt to you in full measure all at once? It just isn't, no matter how much you confess or believe for it. It has never been that way in the Bible.

The first thing is that God has to establish something in your life. *You are going to have to trust Him*, and give Him reason to trust you. It's a two-way communication. You can't say out one side of your mouth one day that you trust God and the next day say, *Where is it?* You have to get to the point where you walk in the will and the Word of God and never waver from it, because Jesus tells us that a double-minded man can't receive anything. Nothing. That's right, not even a little bit, because he is so confused he can't grab onto anything and hold it. (James 1:6-8).

Have you ever exercised your faith for something and then lost it? Well, when you're not fully grounded in the Word, things just either never come to pass or else you lose them when they do come to pass. They fall out of your hand, because you're not steady yet. When you are faithful in little things, and when that steadiness develops in you and your faith is working, God will reward you with big things. I mean great big things, large things. And your faith will be developed so you can hold what He gives you as a vision.

When you are willing to go minister to just a few people instead of just thinking about public ministry before hundreds or thousands, then God can move you up. After all, ministry is to anybody besides you, to anyone outside your own private worship.

WORKING WITH THE SPIRIT
...

Today the Holy Spirit comes differently than He did in the Old Testament, and His work isn't always in a glory cloud. That's only one manifestation of His presence. You have the Holy Ghost inside you, and He has gifts. So whenever you need His gifts, they manifest. The Bible says those gifts manifest as He wills, but I don't think the only way to read that is that it is as God wills.

I think man's will has something to do with it, too. God is also talking about what man wills. I know this may go against what you have been taught or heard, but remain open with me as we continue in truth. People have lost out of the miraculous happening in their lives for so long by saying God wasn't willing when they just didn't want to go the whole mile.

The Holy Ghost always wills to deliver people, to set them free, to break up their bondage. It's always God's will. But the Holy Ghost won't move if you won't move with Him, because you are His vessel on this earth.

You really need to understand that. Stop and hang onto it for a minute and let it get inside you. You aren't going to manipulate the Holy Ghost, but you are His vessel on the earth. He's got to have you to move, and if you aren't willing, He's not going to be able to move. When He finds out that He can't depend on you to move when He keeps telling you, then He goes on to someone who is willing to be used. If God could have done it without you, He would never have sent Jesus. He wouldn't have needed a body in the first place. He would have just sent the Holy Ghost.

Do you see it? It's as you will. As you will to meet the needs of people, as that's your real DESIRE, then the Holy Ghost will flow through you and all of the gifts of the Holy Spirit will be there at the time you need them to arise for help.

Once you are called and appointed for the service God has called you to, you become a candidate for the anointing of God. This anointing is a special outpouring of the power of God to accomplish a task that He appoints you to do. I can tell you right now: you won't accomplish your task without the anointing of God.

You can be a singer, or a preacher, or a teacher, but you won't accomplish the task God has called and appointed you to do without the anointing that goes along with it. But you can be assured that God won't appoint you to a task without giving you the ability to do it. You hear it everywhere that *it's the Word of God that's anointed*. The Word of God *is* anointed, but it's the Word and the Spirit that work together.

You have to understand that the anointing becomes stronger when stronger faith is placed in it. Even though there is a special anointing that accompanies the Word as it is going forth, it will only be manifested in the fullness of God's power when you expect that anointing to work in you. The more you rely on it and lean on it, the stronger it is going to grow.

You may see that anointing in measure, but you won't see it in great measure in unbelieving congregations. God is not going to waste His gifts and time on people who don't care about Him.

When we went to South Africa, we preached, and the people just believed everything we said from the Word. If you can show it to them in the Bible, they will believe it. They had never heard the Bible preached like that. They had never heard just the Bible preached. They had heard a bunch of junk and doctrine, but not just the Word of God— at least not where we went. They just believed it when they heard they were healed by Jesus' stripes, and the sick and crippled got up and walked away healed.

One woman was told that she was going to die, but the Spirit of God rose up on the inside of me and I said, "It's a lie from the devil. God is going to heal you right now. Stand up here." I sang to her, and she was completely healed. She had leukemia, and she was completely restored. We have so many testimonies like that, both from foreign countries and from this country.

It is the anointing that breaks the yoke, just like the Bible says, but how many of you have been in services where either the one ministering isn't anointed, or the people don't care about it? When people have heard this doctrine or that doctrine for so long, no matter what God does, even if He did ten miracles, all the response you'd get would be *Well, that would be nice.* There won't be an anointing in a situation like that, because God won't waste it on them.

God wants His will to be done, and He will find someone who will do it. He'll look for ones who want to receive from Him. So you have to prepare in your own life, and you have to prepare the people wherever you go to benefit from the anointing.

THE GROUNDWORK:
UNITY AND FAITHFULNESS
· · ·

In the Scriptures we looked at above, including 2 Chronicles 5, we saw that the groundwork had been laid by years of preparation in the lives of those men before David appointed them. They had been faithful to do what David told them to do. Now, at the dedication of the temple, the glory came down.

How does this apply today? Let's look at what the Word says they did to get that anointing working in their lives. For one thing, they were all in one accord. Look at that passage again, and you'll see that they were all in one accord. There wasn't any division among them.

> **And when the trumpeters and singers were joined in unison, making one sound to be heard in praising and thanking the Lord....**
>
> 2 Chronicles 5:13

You see, it doesn't matter what position you hold in the kingdom of God as far as any authority that you have or any designated task that you have been given goes. What matters is that you are sanctified before God, that you are purified in heart, and that among the believers there is no division. You are just like the janitor of the church or the pastor. There is no division in the Spirit. God doesn't look on you with more respect than He does anyone else. So you shouldn't see differences either, even if people have different callings and tasks. All of us have to be holy and humble before God.

When the Word says that these men were in unison praising the Lord, that doesn't mean musical unison; that they just hummed around until they finally hit a note together. It doesn't mean they played different songs until they found one they liked. They were in unison—spirit, soul and body. What they were doing unto the Lord was a reflection of their single-mindedness, their one-mindedness, their complete unity. They were sealed together.

When they came together, there was no division. It was as if a single person was standing there doing the praising. They just melted together, strong and tight in the love of the Lord. It was then that they lifted their voices and instruments

48

to sing praise to God, declaring His goodness and mercy forever. Then the House of the Lord was filled with a cloud.

Where were their hearts? They were in God. That is where they had put their treasure. That is where they put their praise and worship. They actually had one heart. God was in their presence, and He manifested His power to them because of their willingness to go forth first and praise and thank Him for it. They believed Him.

The purpose of the praisers and worshippers was to remind the people that God's mercy and lovingkindness endure forever. You see, they had been through a time when it didn't look like God was there. But they praised God continually, to remind themselves and others that God's mercy and lovingkindness were forever.

They were constantly attacked from both within and without. The enemy was continually trying to consume them and to put out their light, but as long as they praised and worshipped God, their light never went out.

Because of their faithfulness to praise Him, there were a lot of battles they never had to fight. Once the ministry of praise and worship is going, the anointing of God is free to break loose and God will manifest Himself. It's always the same. You'll see the things of God if you get people to come into unity in worship and praise.

Faithfulness to do what God tells you to do is another way to see Him work. If you want a captive audience, a prison is a good place to go. The only problem is that none of the prisoners are glad you came if they're not saved. But I tell you, there is nothing more thrilling than going into prisons. We have gone into prisons all over the country, and the gifts of the Holy Ghost really come alive in prisons.

On July 4, 1976, Bill went into a prison to preach on freedom. Isn't it great how the Holy Ghost sets things up? What better day for a gospel message on freedom in Jesus than Independence Day? We have created holidays to remind us of things we ought to remember all the time. Well, on this day we decided to give up the fireworks and go to the prison.

While Bill was preaching, the anointing was so strong on him that even the hard-core criminals were weeping. He wasn't giving an altar call or anything, just preaching under the anointing. He saw three people in white clothes sitting in the back—he thought they might be cafeteria workers because they had long hair and were dressed in white. But he also noticed that they were really big. I mean Bill is no small guy, but sitting down, these people were BIG. Bill was distracted by the fact that their clothes weren't just white, but were brilliant.

No one else saw them except Bill, and as he spoke they confirmed what he preached. They would look at each other and nod, and then they would stare straight ahead. God confirms His anointed Word in a lot of ways.

Twice I have seen a cloud descend over the people to the extent that I couldn't see anything, and I wanted to go with that cloud when it left. Do you have any idea what I mean? Well, God wouldn't let me. He wanted me to continue what I was doing. I just wanted to lay down and go to sleep and disappear in that cloud. But God said, *No, I want you to continue. I'm doing something here.* It was all I could do to stand in the middle of it.

Those days are coming more and more as we are faithful, diligent and unified in spirit, soul and body. But one of the reasons we don't see it is that we don't believe it. We don't prepare ourselves for God to move, and we don't really respect His work enough. We would like to see it and get caught up in the goose bumps when it happens. We would probably even talk about it all week. But what happens the other three weeks of the month? The other months of the year?

We must separate ourselves once and for all from this world and its contaminating influences and renew our minds daily to the Word of Truth.

In church services, Christians shouldn't be the ones coming forward to get healed. They should be walking in divine health. There is no reason for them not to, except due to a lack of knowledge. The Bible says that God's people perish for lack of knowledge, and so they perish. The hospitals are full of perishing Christians.

Until the life of the Christian is so obviously different from the life of the sinner, why should the sinner want what the Christian has? The anointing needs to flow for those people to come to God.

Today in churches, musicians suffer from much the same problem. They're all worn out before they get to the service and have to use their faith just to stand there and play or sing. They feel blessed if they get to sing a song or two before the preacher cuts them off. If they get a little too carried away, then praise is over, and the service moves on to announcements or something else. That is why we don't see God move.

It's so good when God moves that people don't care how long they stay. In Africa we would minister for four or five hours in a church. It was nothing—the people just wouldn't go home. You couldn't get them to go home. Some had walked for miles and some for days to get to the service. They really wanted to know and learn about God.

They brought their food, and they ate and slept right there on the floor. They didn't care. They weren't going to leave until they got from God what they needed. Until you are determined to get from God what He has to give you, you aren't going to see that glory cloud. When you get one heart, one mind, one attitude, just as if you had one body—even if it's in a small group of people—you'll see things happen.

The purpose of this unity isn't just to get a great blessing, but so your life will be so saturated with that glory that when you see people on the street they'll know something is different, and they'll feel the anointing of God. We can't keep coming to church to learn the Word and forget it when we're with sinners. We believe it...then we doubt it. Then we expect it to work for us. Remember, the covenant of God is for you to share with sinners. Get them in on it!

CHAPTER 4

···

David's Anointing

···

David's Anointing
•••

I want to talk about David, because he was a musician first, and that anointing went over his life into other things as God called and set him in the highest offices of the nation of Israel—the office of prophet and king.

Like a lot of musicians, David developed a skill and then he answered God's call on his life. While he was tending sheep, he played his lyre or harp. He sang songs unto the Lord and got himself musically prepared. He didn't know what he was preparing for, but he applied himself to what he was doing.

He didn't have any idea the glory of God was going to come upon him in such a way. He was just a little shepherd boy. But he loved God and sang to Him out of the abundance of his heart day after day. He was just preparing to have the call of God on his life fulfilled, and once he was ready, he was appointed to the task.

In First Samuel 16 we see how the Lord took notice of David's love and devotion and also of his diligent preparation and sent Samuel to anoint him. It's interesting, isn't it, that God didn't even tell His own prophet who it was going to be, except that it was one of Jesse's sons. He had to be led by the Spirit, too.

So Samuel went to Bethlehem to find the one he was supposed to anoint. Jesse must have had a good looking crew. They must have been really strong-looking men. That outward appearance almost fooled even Samuel. He walked up and down and looked at them. He looked over their physiques, and boy, they looked just right. Each one of them looked like a king.

Can't you just see these big, strong, handsome men? They looked like they would be mighty men of valor, but God kept Samuel moving down the line. *No, not him.* That must have puzzled Samuel. Finally he asked Jesse, "Is that all your sons?" And Jesse said, "No, I have another boy, my youngest, but he's down tending sheep. He's just a boy, not even a man yet. I didn't want to bother him."

Don't you know that when Samuel saw him, he was looking through the eyes of God? When you are prepared to do something and you are obeying God like Samuel was, you're about to be the vessel for the anointing of God on somebody else.

You know that had to be exciting for Samuel when he laid his hands upon David and poured the oil over him and anointed him to be king. David had reddish hair, fair skin and beautiful eyes. He was fine-looking.

The Lord spoke to Samuel and confirmed what rose up inside him:

> **Jesse sent and brought him. David had a healthy reddish complexion and beautiful eyes,**

**and was fine-looking. The Lord said [to Samuel],
Arise, anoint him; this is he.**

1 Samuel 16:12

Notice that Samuel didn't rely on what he thought in the natural. He didn't argue with God and say, *I can't see this kid being king. He's too young to have that kind of wisdom. He's not mature enough. Can't we just put him on the back row for a couple of years and let him grow into these things?* God said, "This is the one," and that was all he needed to go on.

The Word doesn't say the others were jealous or anything. Now you can imagine in the natural, that Samuel pouring oil on the youngest brother must have lifted a few eyebrows among the older ones. But Samuel was a man after God's own heart, and he just went ahead and did what God told him to do without worrying about what people might think.

You'll have to do the same thing when God calls, appoints and anoints you for a task. What God wants is never going to please everybody if they haven't already made a commitment to be in agreement with what He wants and not with what they want.

Samuel set his face like a flint to do God's Word, and guess what happened to David? Verse 13 tells us that **the Spirit of the Lord came mightily upon David from that day forward.** He was a changed young man. It happens to everyone who is called out and anointed by God.

After being called, appointed and anointed by God, David's first appointment was in music.

Saul's servants said to him, Behold, an evil
spirit from God torments you.

Let our lord now command your servants here
before you to find a man who plays skillfully on
the lyre; and when the evil spirit from God is upon
you, he will play it, and you will be well.

Saul told his servants, Find me a man who
plays well and bring him to me.

One of the young men said, I have seen a son
of Jesse the Bethlehemite who plays skillfully, a
valiant man, a man of war, prudent in speech and
eloquent, an attractive person; and the Lord is
with him.

So Saul sent messengers to Jesse, and said,
Send me David your son, who is with the sheep.

And Jesse took a donkey loaded with bread, a
skin of wine, and a kid, and sent them by David his
son to Saul.

And David came to Saul and served him. Saul
became very fond of him, and he became his
armor-bearer.

Saul sent to Jesse, saying, Let David remain in
my service, for he pleases me.

And when the evil spirit from God was upon
Saul, David took a lyre and played it; so Saul was
refreshed and became well, and the evil spirit
left him.

1 Samuel 16:15-23

There are some things to look at carefully here. First of
all, they were looking for someone who played skillfully.
Then someone remembered what he had seen in David. He
saw exactly what God saw. God saw a skillful man, a man of
courage, a man who could communicate well. He could

express what was inside of him. Besides all that, he was good-looking.

What you want to pay attention to, however, is that David didn't know who was watching him when he played. That wasn't what he was aiming for, to promote himself. You never know who is watching you while you're preparing yourself to do tasks God has called you to.

The whole area was familiar with David, though: they all knew what he did. They could hear him playing, and as they walked along, his music floated through the evening air, or across the valleys in the afternoons while he kept sheep. They knew he was good. Your ears just tell you when someone is skillful and gifted. So David was sent for, and he found favor in the sight of the king.

The living Word is being exalted and drawing men and women from every walk of life to Himself. So if you are called, keep preparing both your heart and your natural abilities. If you are faithful in the small things and do not misuse the anointing, then God will lift you up. You will be called on to minister to people in high places.

When David played, the anointing became so strong that it broke the yoke that tried to hold Saul. Saul could have gotten rid of it entirely if he had purposed in his heart to abide solely by God's Word, and not be an off-again-on-again man. But he wouldn't do that. He was double-minded. You don't receive anything when you're double-minded. But David ministered deliverance to him through his music. Deliverance is one of the functions of anointed music.

As Christians, we have had a religious tradition of looking back at Old Testament heroes like David and saying, *Wow, David was a great man. I wish I could do something like that.* Remember that even the men who were in the army were afraid of Goliath and their fear kept them from being used of God. In their own minds, they saw themselves as losing the battle. That was their vision, so they were bound by it.

David never carried that kind of a vision in his whole life. He had such a trust in and such a love for God all his life that all he ever saw was victory.

We should be exactly like David, and we ought to expect even greater miracles, because we have the same God and an even better covenant with Him. All David could do was to cry out, "Who are you to rise up against God's chosen people; Who do you think you are?" The Philistine said to David, "Come on pipsqueak. I'm going to give your flesh to the birds." Can't you just hear that giant roaring? He really roared in laughter, too. That had to be the biggest joke of the day: a shepherd boy coming out against a giant. So the Philistines let their guard down, and they got slaughtered.

That's the way it is in battle. Even if you've got a better weapon, which we do with God, if you let your guard down, you're still going to get killed. Notice that David didn't rely on his natural abilities or courage, though. He was relying on the Word and the name of his God.

Then said David to the Philistine, You come to me with a sword, a spear, and a javelin, but I come

**to you in the name of the Lord of hosts, the God of
the ranks of Israel, Whom you have defied.**
1 Samuel 17:45

Everybody knows victory speeches are made *after* the
victory. David knew he already had the victory because of
God's Word.

**The Lord shall cause your enemies who rise
up against you to be defeated before your face;
they shall come out against you one way and flee
before you seven ways.**
Deuteronomy 28:7

You see, that was David's guarantee. That was the Word
of God coming out of his mouth, because he knew who he
was to his God. He knew God wasn't about to leave him or
forsake him. He had a vision of that kind of a God.

Do you know why he had that kind of a vision all the
time? Because all he did was meditate on the Word all day
long. All he did was sing about it. All he did was serve God.
That was all he did. That's why he could have such a vision.

You can have that vision, that faith image of your Father
and of yourself in Jesus if you meditate on it all the time.
There is no reason not to expect the power of God to be
manifest in our lives if we believe what He says about us.

Satan will come to you with hard talk about failure,
especially if you've made a mistake or are in debt or if you've
never learned to trust in God. So your Goliath may be
someone coming to take away your car. It may be a payment
you can't make. Who are they to rise up against God's
anointed? God didn't give you His covenant so you could
stand up in front of someone and strut, but He did give it so

you could be bold in the face of every circumstance that Satan brings against you.

God gave that covenant so the world would know that it's the God who created heaven and the earth that you serve. He is the God whose power you're standing in, and He's not going to be mocked or made fun of. Neither are His children, especially when they are His servants.

You see, God already won all the physical battles when He lived out a human life through His Son in Jesus' body. So that's all taken care of. We've been given all things that pertain to life and godliness, and we have been blessed with all spiritual blessings in heavenly places. (2 Peter 1:3; Ephesians 1:3). So the only battle left is the one waged in your mind.

You hear the battle happening in your head. *You're not going to make it. Yes, you are. No, you're not. I'll stand. No, you'll fall. I'm healed. I don't feel like it. I can't see my prosperity.*

On and on your mind reels until you finally believe God. And then all the lies that the principalities and powers try to put in your mind just become transparent to you, and all you can see is God's promise standing on the other side of the smokescreen, and you go get it.

Here's what David said to this giant:

> **And all this assembly shall know that the Lord saves not with sword and spear; for the battle is the Lord's and He will give you into our hands.**
>
> **1 Samuel 17:47**

When the giant ran forward to meet him, David ran quickly to meet the enemy. Who won? Was it prophesied? It wasn't a physical battle even though David held the slingshot and killed the giant. He didn't do it out of fear, did he? He did it because he knew God was going to deliver the giant into his hands. David knew his authority in the binding covenant God had given him.

COVENANT BATTLES
...

I want to relate the truths of David's story to you in terms of incidents I know about and that you can probably relate to even better.

You have to really know your authority and lean on the anointing whenever you go into areas where evil spirits have been the ruler. They like to be in control of things, and when you go into their territory and start slicing them up and kicking them out of their homes, they start making a lot of noise, trying to destroy the peace and break up meetings. They try to keep it so stirred up that nobody will understand anything from God or hear anything. You had better go in there with revelation knowledge concerning your authority.

God has appointed you and has given you spiritual authority to do the job. So all you have to do is wield your sword with the authority in it, using it skillfully. You just have to remember that it's a spiritual battle and not a physical one. You've got to understand that it's not the person you're coming against. You have to be walking in your spiritual authority when you go out on the street to preach, because you'll have every opportunity to be in a fight, a physical one, not just a spiritual one.

One night when Bill and I were in Minneapolis for a convention, we went out on the street in a section that's a lot like New Orleans. Everything the devil has was there: bars, prostitution and homosexuality on the streets, people selling everything from dope to watches, gangs and hoodlums, a lot of weird stuff. God told us to sit and observe some things. We sat inside a windowsill on a street corner.

There was a young man standing a few yards off preaching the Word of God. He was preaching on the corner. He was a small guy, and he didn't look like he had a lot of money, much education or anything. He just knew God. You could tell that he knew God. He was jumping up and down, preaching repentance and salvation and the love of God. He was excited about what he was saying. He wasn't preaching damnation; it was the good news he was preaching.

As he began to preach and as the Word began to go forth stronger and stronger, a circle formed around him, not of people, but a circle of empty space where people would skirt around him. The sidewalk wasn't that wide, and the people would walk out in the street to get around him. At first they were just brushing by to get around him, but as the anointing of God kept getting stronger and stronger, they circled him from afar. They couldn't even get close to him. They couldn't even touch him.

Then I saw a man across the street. He was muttering and pacing back and forth, charging himself up. He would point at the preacher across the street and tell everybody to look at him. The little preacher had his back to him and would jump up and down as the anointing got stronger. This big guy had a fist that looked as big as a bowling ball. I felt like I was watching a movie.

I knew God wanted to teach me something as I was sitting there watching. The preacher didn't know what was going on across the street, because he was lost in God's love for the people and God's desire to get them saved. But he obviously knew his authority in Jesus.

The big guy started across the street, and he was walking at such a slant I don't know how he stood up. He looked like he was walking up a hill where he could almost touch it with his nose. It really looked like a cartoon.

He looked top-heavy as he walked, with fists like bowling balls. I knew he meant to kill the guy preaching. One hit and it would have been over. I wondered who was going to get up and take his place. I was trying to say something to Bill, and he was saying, "I'd better go get that guy." Bill's no sissy, and he wanted to help the preacher. But God wouldn't let either one of us up. We were nailed to our seats, watching.

Everybody across the street was going "Woo, Woo," and pointing at the guy winding up as he came. The preacher never even turned around or quit preaching but lifted his arm back toward the intruder and just pointed his finger and said, "In the name of Jesus!"

Boom! The man was about 10 feet away and fell down flat. Then everybody across the street went, "Wow!" And then the circle got bigger around the preacher.

You know the anointing of God was there to accomplish the task, and the young preacher really believed in it. He wasn't afraid of anything or anybody. If he had gotten into a physical fight, he would have been killed. But it's the things you don't see that count, not what you do see. It isn't just a physical world you're living in. You've got to see yourself as a spirit being in a spirit world where the battles are spiritual battles. You can win the spiritual battles, but you won't win the physical ones if that's where you try to do your warfare.

> **For we are not wrestling with flesh and blood [contending only with physical opponents], but against the despotisms, against the powers, against [the master spirits who are] the world rulers of this present darkness, against the spirit forces of wickedness in the heavenly (supernatural) sphere.**
>
> Ephesians 6:12

> **For the weapons of our warfare are not physical [weapons of flesh and blood], but they are mighty before God for the overthrow and destruction of strongholds.**
>
> 2 Corinthians 10:4

What the young preacher on the streets did was just another illustration of what David did before Goliath. He knew his covenant and his spiritual authority in the name of his God. Jesus' name rules our world, and when we receive revelation of who He is, we rule in His name in confidence and power and victory.

You will have that vision of Him before you if you are doing what David did, meditating, singing, thinking about His Word all day long. David was constantly in God's covenant Word. If you'll learn to think on God, even difficult or intense jobs will get easier.

You'll get a vision of who you are in this world and of what you are sent out to do. Nobody will shake it from you. Nobody can take anything from you unless you give them an open door. Staying, abiding in the Word makes that an impossibility. David played the Word, sang the Word and abode in the Word all the time. That's why he was so successful.

> **This Book of the Law shall not depart out of your mouth, but you shall meditate on it day and night, that you may observe and do according to all that is written in it. For then you shall make your way prosperous, and then you shall deal wisely and have good success.**
>
> **Joshua 1:8**

The devil walks around only looking for those who will give him permission to devour them. If you let him, he'll do it. We looked up the word *devour* in the Greek, and it means *to drink down*. He doesn't have any teeth to chew on you with. He has to break you down little by little and dissolve you to the point where he can drink you down, because he can't chew you up.

Let me give you an example of a woman who lost the covenant battle. I was in Illinois, and the meeting was going to be canceled because there was a blizzard outside, and you couldn't see anything. A man I knew asked me if I would go with him to minister to his mother. God told me to go and sing to her and comfort her, because she was dying of cancer.

We arrived there, and as soon as we walked into the house, the smell of death and evil tried to overtake me. I almost vomited, it smelled so bad. You do know that death smells bad, don't you? It's evil, nauseating. I get mad when I have to smell the devil's work.

I sat in the living room and prayed for about an hour and just thought on the things of the Lord. Then I went into the bedroom and told her God wanted to offer her something today. Weakly she asked, "What's that?"

I said, "Life. It's up to you to choose it. You can have it if you want it. He will bring you up out of the bed if you desire. He wants me to sing deliverance to you." I sang to her, and I ministered to her.

As I was singing to her, God told me she had dry rot of the bones. I asked her son, "What's her condition?" He said, "She has cancer of the bones." The Word says the dry rot of the bones is caused by envy and jealousy.

Did you know there are causes for diseases?

Do not be deceived and deluded and misled; God will not allow Himself to be sneered at (scorned, disdained or mocked by mere pretensions or professions, or by His precepts being set aside). [He inevitably deludes himself who attempts to delude God]. For whatever a man sows, that and that only is what he will reap.

Galatians 6:7

Why do you think we are being taught so much about the fact that we are going to have what we say? Most people don't take it seriously, because if they did, they wouldn't say many of the things they do. If you plant weeds in the lives of others as well as in your own, you'll reap those weeds.

People with cancer, mental oppression, or other diseases, have just reaped the weeds that they have sown, or that they didn't pull up when someone else sowed them. Sooner or later, the seeds of what you say are going to manifest into fruit, good or rotten.

As I continued to praise God by that woman's bed, the spirit of grief tried to come on me and attach itself to me. When it came on me I knew in my heart that she wasn't going to turn from what had bound her. She was so beaten down by the devil, she couldn't even eat. She couldn't physically hold anything down.

It was just a matter of time before she went on home, a Spirit-filled, born-again Christian who had been devoured by the devil. She left a 9-year-old boy, an older son, a husband and grandchildren behind her. That wasn't God's will.

It is hard for those people to grow up and understand God. It puts a stumbling block in their lives for them to have faith in God.

I was going to minister to her, but she didn't want to be delivered. She enjoyed the singing, and she loved God, but the devil had broken her down and she had just quit. Sometimes God will tell you not to do it when you pray for someone. They have made a choice with their mouths to go another way.

I've had warning after warning from God about a man who isn't going to keep on living a lot longer because he is shooting himself with a gun. The Lord told me that he is committing suicide with his mouth. Everyday he is filling himself with bullet holes by what he says. His confession runs something like, "He meets all my needs, but I have to work my tail off to get it." And "Oh yeah, God will heal me." But he goes to the hospital to have surgery after surgery.

Those seeds of thoughtless resistance to God's Word keep growing and spreading out until they take over your soul and finally your body. You need to understand that to say things which contradict the Word of God is to mock God, and you can't do that and prosper. The Word of God just isn't going to work for you like that, because you aren't taking it seriously.

CHAPTER 5

...

From That Day Forward

...

C H A P T E R   5

From That Day Forward
• • •

I began talking about David's anointing because I wanted to show you that God's laws and ways don't change. That's true about the anointing, too. There are prophets anointed by God today just as much as Samuel was a prophet anointed by God then. We don't worship men, but we do reverence and respect them for their faithfulness, and the knowledge and wisdom which they have gained by working with and knowing God a lot longer than most of us—longer than many of us have been alive.

But the particular point I'm after concerns what God's Word says happened to David when he was anointed. The Spirit of God came on him mightily, *from that day forward*, and *he was a different person*. The same thing happened to me, and I want to tell you about it and what happened to my ministry after that.

God has called me into the ministry of a psalmist, and I was preparing, studying and serving in my apprenticeship, and had gone out and ministered as if I were a full-fledged psalmist. I was acting as one, but I didn't have full knowledge or understanding of that ministry. But I headed myself in that direction as well as I could. Still, there wasn't a full measure there.

I had reached a point where I was so frustrated in my life that I just resigned my position as a worker in the kingdom of God. I was upset because nothing was happening. I knew God had called me, but I really didn't know what I was. I knew there was more to it than being a singer, and it made me mad when people called me a singer. I couldn't figure out what was going on.

What released me into doing what God called me to do was that God sent me into the path of one of His prophets. When the man of God laid his hands on me, he said the Lord had told him that a new anointing would come on me.

What happened was that I was not only encouraged and stirred up in my spirit, but something like a veil was taken away. I could see more clearly what I was to do and how the anointing works when I minister. My responsibility is to hold what He gave me and to move on. Whenever God has something more for me, the veil on the next thing will be taken away. What God doesn't want is for any of us to misuse His anointing and so lose it. I must continue to study and show myself approved, a workman who has no need of being ashamed.

When God sees that you are continually seeking Him, continually undoing the devil's works with His word, loosing the bonds of wickedness, undoing heavy burdens, setting the oppressed free, taking off their yokes, and above all, putting the needs of others first, then God will move you into a different realm. I don't really care what comes next. All I care about is doing what is in front of me with great diligence and attention. When I'm found to be a trustworthy servant, then I'll be promoted. God always checks our hearts.

I want to point out, though, that the anointing opened up to me when a man of God laid his hands on me. That doesn't mean that you should run around looking for someone to lay hands on you. It means you should do everything else first, and God will send that to you if it becomes necessary for you. You might just take hold of the Word, and it takes hold of you, and you go right into what you're supposed to do. I'm not giving a formula but sharing an experience that points to the importance of the anointing for ministry. The anointing comes directly from God, but it can be restored into our spirits in a lot of ways.

After receiving that anointing, I really began to see God work in my ministry. For example, we had started a church in Franklin, Tennessee and before we left, a young man and his wife from John Osteen's church had to come up to take over as pastors. They had just stepped into full-time ministry. You couldn't find anybody more willing to serve God than they were. But something wasn't working for them. They were standing on the Word, and everybody was praying and interceding for them. Still, there was a yoke of some kind on them. It seemed to me like something was clinging on like an octopus with tentacles, and even if you cut them off, they grew right back.

I was waiting on God one day when He said, *It will be all right. The circumstances seem higher than the Word but I want you to take your guitar to their house, sit in their living room with them and sing to them.* I'd never done that before, so I said, *Are you kidding?* In my natural mind I was hearing all the rationalizations that keep you from doing what God wants and from getting the victory. I thought, *Boy, they're in trouble, Father, and you want me to sing a couple of songs to them?* Everything was wrong for them.

I argued for a while, *Do you want me to go over there while they're building on their house and putting in insulation that will keep them from freezing and tell them, "Hey guys, God told me to come over and sing to you?" Is that what you want me to do?* All the way over there I was going over and over it. But God can get real silent when He wants you to act on what He says without having a lot of reason for doing it.

I just made up my mind to do it though, because I had been listening to testimonies from men like Norvel Hayes and Kenneth Copeland about obedience. The Holy Spirit would tell them to do something; they would go do it and see great results. I thought, *I'm going to do that. I wonder if anything like that would ever happen in my life?* I asked myself, *Why doesn't that ever happen to me?* I got an answer from God, *You would never go and do the things I tell you to do that sound foolish. You always rebuke them.*

I knew a man who was really good at obeying that way. He was a pizza maker. He had a big factory, too. One day God told him to go downtown and stand on a particular street corner. He walked down there and waited. Then God said, *There's a man coming around the corner any minute.* He told him what the man would be wearing and told him that when he saw the man cross the street to go to him and say, "Today God sent me here to ask you to invite Him into your life."

When he saw him coming he went over and introduced himself and told him that God had sent him to tell him that he needed to give his life to God today. They were walking across the street, and the man fell down. Kablam! Right in the street on his knees, and accepted Jesus. The traffic stopped, they cried and hugged each other, and the man was eternally saved.

I wanted that kind of anointing on my life. I wanted to go do those things and see great things happen. So God told me that if I would start doing what He said, no matter how off-the-wall it sounded, He'd give it to me.

When you start playing your music, that's what you learn. You learn to listen to God while you are playing in front of a few. You have no idea what is going to happen. You may change millions of lives through one person. You don't know who that man was that heard you or what he might do. He may turn out to be a great evangelist.

As it turned out with the couple from Franklin, Tennessee, I went to their house, and they were embarrassed. But we sat down and I started to sing, acting clamorously foolish just to get myself loose and to loosen them up. Then I sang for about thirty minutes, and they started to sink down in their chairs and really soak in the blessings and the refreshing of the Spirit of God. I was there a couple of hours and at the end we were all just caught up in praise and worship of God.

But do you know what? The yoke was broken, and every situation in their lives changed. We ended that time with a laughing party, because we knew that the evil spirit that had been assigned to them was gone for good. They were completely free.

From then on, I would do that with people as God would instruct me. You have to be obedient to move with God, though, or you might get stopped or let resentment grow up in your heart that will allow the devil to frustrate you. He always works little by little against your obedience until He can wear you out, like that woman with cancer. Then he can drink you down.

You would be surprised, but people can get so discouraged that they say, "Well, I love God, but I can't mess around with this faith stuff. I can't walk like they are talking."

It will be all over when you come to that point. You will never live out your days, and you'll never finish what God has called you to do.

Just make up your mind to be like David. He stood up against a giant that scared everybody else and said what was in his heart, because he knew his God.

THE POWER OF THE GLORY
• • •

I want to talk about another of the greatest victories of music and praise in the Old Testament.

In Second Chronicles 20, Jehoshaphat was faced with circumstances that were impossible to overcome by natural means. So he cried out to God. He and all the people were waiting on God together. They got in agreement in a hurry when it looked like they were about to be wiped out. (I think some churches would have to come to that point to get in agreement.)

What was going to happen? One of the prophets stood up and spoke what was going to happen, telling the people God's Word. "Don't be afraid, because this battle isn't yours." The exhortation began to soothe everybody. God had told them not only *what* was going to happen, but *how* to do it.

> Be not afraid or dismayed at this great multitude; for the battle is not yours, but God's.
>
> Tomorrow go down to them. Behold, they will come up by the Ascent of Ziz, and you will find them at the end of the ravine before the Wilderness of Jeruel.
>
> You shall not need to fight in this battle; take your positions, stand still, and see the deliverance of the Lord [Who is] with you, O Judah and Jerusalem. Fear not nor be dismayed. Tomorrow go out against them, for the Lord is with you.
>
> 2 Chronicles 20:15-17

God was telling them, *I want you to see what I can do. Just take your stand.* Never get so haphazard about your authority that you don't go out for the battles; but when you go out, go out with the authority of your knowledge about who is doing the fighting. Your part is to stand still in the middle of it all and watch Him work.

The Word of the Lord came through the prophets then—that is why they had to believe the prophets to prosper. If you stand fast on God's Word when it comes to you, you'll prosper, too.

Jehoshaphat was a man of God, in that he put God first. So when he heard the Word of God, he acted on it. He told the people that they could rely on God's Word, and then he consulted them.

> When he had consulted with the people, he appointed singers to sing to the Lord and praise Him in their holy [priestly] garments as they went out before the army, saying, Give thanks to the Lord, for His mercy and loving-kindness endure forever!
>
> And when they began to sing and to praise, the Lord set ambushments against the men of Ammon, Moab, and Mount Seir, who had come against Judah, and they were [self-] slaughtered;
>
> For [suspecting betrayal] the men of Ammon and Moab rose against those of Mount Seir, utterly destroying them. And when they had made an end of the men of Seir, they all helped to destroy one another.
>
> 2 Chronicles 20:21-23

They had the battle plan, and even before the battle, they went out celebrating the victory. You can imagine that they had to choose whether they would believe the Word of the prophet or not. But there was no wavering in them, and they worshipped God as soon as they heard the Word. And the next day, all the way to the battle they were worshipping and praising Him.

The really important point I want to make about this story is that there is only an anointing from God when you are doing what He has told you to do, and that anointing is only there to accomplish one thing—the task God sent it to do. That's the only reason the anointing comes. Obedience and trust cause that anointing to flow.

The importance of the story of Jehoshaphat's ordeal is that the people believed God, praised and worshipped Him, and their faith caused the anointing of the Holy Spirit to come on their behalf.

Look closely at what they did. They hooked up. They started to flow with that anointing and started going toward the battle with God's anointing. I believe that their faith, praise and obedience caused a glory cloud that looked like fog to come down over those armies early in the morning, and the enemy got confused and fearful and started to kill each other off.

When they had completely wiped each other out, God lifted His glory cloud off them, and when Israel got there, all they could see for miles were dead bodies. Whenever the glory of God comes down, the works of the enemy are killed. That's how God's presence works.

That is the attitude we should always have—our whole lifestyle is our reasonable form of worship. (Romans 12:1). You know who God is and what His character and nature are, so you can just thank Him that all the battles are already won and all you have to do is worship and adore Him—stay in His presence where nothing can get to you. If you stay in the glory of God, anything that tries to come against you is coming against the glory of God, and nothing and nobody can do that and succeed.

The truth we have to get hold of in the body of Christ is that *the anointing of God is always available.* That anointing will always undo the works and the designs of the devil. *The anointing of God is in his Word....All power to accomplish what He has said is within his Word.* (Hebrews 1:3; Ephesians 1:19-20).

CHAPTER 6

•••

Taking the Word Seriously

•••

Taking the Word Seriously
•••

Until you are ready to respect the things of God and His Word, God really isn't going to be able to entrust you with more than little things. You won't see anything, and you won't have anything. There may be a minor amount of victory and a minor amount of deliverance and a minor appearance of the anointing, but the really great anointing depends upon what the Bible says. Obey the Word, answer your call, develop your skill and spend time in an apprenticeship.

You see, if we want to have God's anointing, we're going to have to be complete believers and doers of the Word, taking God seriously. Then we can expect to walk in His glory. Otherwise, we can forget about it, keep on wishing and hoping, and keep on playing church. God's Word just isn't going to work for people who confess it and don't believe it.

You can only see what you believe by what you are doing with the Word. Once that commitment comes, really comes, into your heart then you're ready to move on to other things. If it doesn't come, there won't be that abundant life God talked about. There will be striving but no flowing. There will be confessing the Word out of one side of your mouth and asking the question, "I wonder where it's coming from?" out of the other.

We must look through the eye of faith to see beyond what the devil has destroyed to victory. It takes an anointing —resulting from faith in God—to raise somebody out of a wheelchair. When we get to the point where we focus on the needs of other people and come together in one spirit, praising God as one, we will see the glory of God.

My confession is that we're getting there. We are going to attain that oneness, and we'll see that it is going to be a common thing. In fact, I believe we'll come to the point that we'll be surprised if it doesn't happen. It used to surprise me when someone got healed in my ministry, but now it surprises me if they don't.

As you praise and worship God, remind both Him and yourself of who He is. *You are great O God Almighty. You are able, and You are willing to do these things in my life.* Remind yourself of who you are in Christ. Prepare your life to be a vessel for the anointing and glory of God, a person with a pure heart, a holy life, a spirit full of and confident in God's Word. Then you, too, will do what He has called you to do. And you'll move moment by moment in God's glory, and the power of God will attend all you do.

Prayer of Salvation

God loves you—no matter who you are, no matter what your past. God loves you so much that He gave His one and only begotten Son for you. The Bible tells us that "...whoever believes in him shall not perish but have eternal life" (John 3:16 NIV). Jesus laid down His life and rose again so that we could spend eternity with Him in heaven and experience His absolute best on earth. If you would like to receive Jesus into your life, say the following prayer out loud and mean it from your heart.

Heavenly Father, I come to You admitting that I am a sinner. Right now, I choose to turn away from sin, and I ask You to cleanse me of all unrighteousness. I believe that Your Son, Jesus, died on the cross to take away my sins. I also believe that He rose again from the dead so that I might be forgiven of my sins and made righteous through faith in Him. I call upon the name of Jesus Christ to be the Savior and Lord of my life. Jesus, I choose to follow You and ask that You fill me with the power of the Holy Spirit. I declare that right now I am a child of God. I am free from sin and full of the righteousness of God. I am saved in Jesus' name. Amen

If you prayed this prayer to receive Jesus Christ as your Savior for the first time, please contact us on the web at www.harrisonhouse.com to receive a free book.

Or you may write to us at
Harrison House Publishers
P.O. Box 35035 • Tulsa, Oklahoma 74153

About the Author

Janny Grein believes music is a universal language that transcends all barriers and captivates the heart of the listener.

From her childhood, Janny has been an overcomer. Even though she had experienced much pain with drugs, alcohol and hustling to stay number one, Janny found acceptance as a musician and songwriter in Nashville.

Her initial efforts were recognized well enough to land a songwriting contract with a major publisher. Her live performances were well attended on the club scene. Yet with all the seeming success, Janny's life was still without purpose or direction. Her songs continued to reflect all her loneliness and longing.

Her life changed one evening at home in April 1975. As Janny and her husband, Bill, watched the Hollywood film, "King of Kings," she realized she needed more: Someone Who would die for her and give up everything for her. That night she found her new life in Jesus Christ, and it would alter her destiny and reshape her life forever.

Janny soon learned that the Word of God is God's will for us today and that it is possible to live an abundant life in His love. Committed to Jesus as her Lord, she began to write songs filled with the joy of her new life.

Many of the songs she has written and recorded are now a part of the strength of the broadcast industry worldwide including: "Bread Upon The Water," "Covenant Woman," "More Than Conquerors," "By His Word," "Stronger Than Before," "Spiritual Freedom" and "Storm of Glory."

From the beginning of her career with Sparrow Records, Janny has been a major influence in the formation and development of contemporary Christian music.

For the past 22 years, Janny has toured 32 countries and the United States conducting concert crusades and sharing her music with millions of listeners. A candid and refreshing personality, she uses her gift of song to communicate the love of Jesus, rekindling dreams and bringing hope into the hearts of people.

Since 1993, Janny has been spreading revival fires to churches in America. By holding extended meetings, she sees God change His people into the image of Christ and strengthen the calling of the pastors. Her tireless pursuit for excellence has taken her to heights beyond her own dreams. Yet her quest continues, and with each new stride of innovation the vision broadens. Her goal is within reach and her focus is stronger than before.

To contact the author, write:

Bill & Janny Grein Ministries
P.O. Box 150959
Fort Worth, TX 76108

or on the web at: www.janny.com

*Please include your prayer requests
and comments when you write.*

Fast. Easy. Convenient.

For the latest Harrison House product information and author news, look no further than your computer. All the details on our powerful, life-changing products are just a click away. New releases, E-mail subscriptions, Podcasts, testimonies, monthly specials—find it all in one place. Visit harrisonhouse.com today!

harrisonhouse

The Harrison House Vision

Proclaiming the truth and the power
Of the Gospel of Jesus Christ
With excellence;

Challenging Christians to
Live victoriously,
Grow spiritually,
Know God intimately.